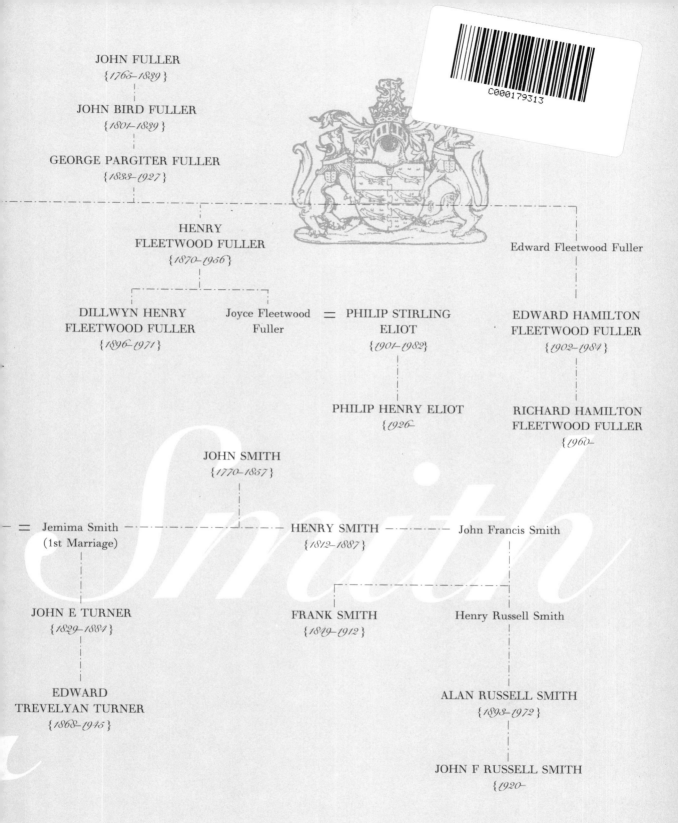

JOHN FULLER
{*1765–1839*}

JOHN BIRD FULLER
{*1801–1839*}

GEORGE PARGITER FULLER
{*1833–1927*}

HENRY
FLEETWOOD FULLER
{*1870–1956*}

Edward Fleetwood Fuller

DILLWYN HENRY
FLEETWOOD FULLER
{*1896–1971*}

Joyce Fleetwood
Fuller

= PHILIP STIRLING
ELIOT
{*1901–1982*}

EDWARD HAMILTON
FLEETWOOD FULLER
{*1902–1984*}

PHILIP HENRY ELIOT
{*1926–*

RICHARD HAMILTON
FLEETWOOD FULLER
{*1960–*

JOHN SMITH
{*1770–1857*}

= Jemima Smith
(1st Marriage)

HENRY SMITH
{*1812–1887*}

John Francis Smith

JOHN E TURNER
{*1829–1881*}

FRANK SMITH
{*1849–1912*}

Henry Russell Smith

EDWARD
TREVELYAN TURNER
{*1868–1945*}

ALAN RUSSELL SMITH
{*1893–1972*}

JOHN F RUSSELL SMITH
{*1920–*

Those involved in the brewery are shown in capital letters.

# LONDON PRIDE

*150 Years of Fuller, Smith & Turner*

# LONDON PRIDE

*150 Years of Fuller, Smith and Turner*

1845-1995

ANDREW LANGLEY

**Good Books**

PRODUCED FOR FULLER, SMITH & TURNER PLC

BY GOOD BOOKS (GB PUBLICATIONS LIMITED)

LAGARD FARM, WHITLEY, MELKSHAM, WILTS SN12 8RL

A CIP CATALOGUE RECORD FOR THE BOOK IS AVAILABLE FROM THE BRITISH LIBRARY.


ISBN 0 946555 37 0


DESIGNED BY DESIGN/SECTION, FROME

COVER DESIGN BY DESIGN HOUSE

COLOUR SEPARATION BY FOTOGRAPHICS LTD, LONDON AND HONG KONG

PRINTED AND BOUND IN SPAIN BY CAYFOSA, BARCELONA


ACKNOWLEDGEMENTS: JACOB KNYFF'S PAINTING "CHISWICK FROM THE RIVER" IS REPRODUCED

BY COURTESY OF THE MUSEUM OF LONDON; THE SOUTH VIEW OF CHISWICK, 1750, COURTESY

OF CHISWICK PUBLIC LIBRARY; MAP OF CHISWICK 1747, COURTESY GUILDHALL LIBRARY,

CORPORATION OF LONDON

FRONTISPIECE: THE BREWERY HOUSE, CHISWICK

# Contents

FOREWORD

BY ANTHONY FULLER CBE

7

1. TWO BREWHOUSES ON THE MALL

9

2. EXIT THOMPSON, ENTER SMITH
AND TURNER

16

3. DISAGREEMENTS AND DEVELOPMENTS

24

4. INTO THE TWENTIETH CENTURY

33

5. FULLER, SMITH & TURNER LIMITED

43

6. THE REAL ALE TRIUMPH

52

# 150 YEARS OF BREWING EXCELLENCE

I would like to introduce to you this new book, which has been produced to commemorate the 150th anniversary of the start of the Fuller, Smith & Turner partnership.

When reading it, you will see that there were many "ups and downs", both in our fortunes and in the relationships between the various partners, going back to the earliest days.

The present company owes a lot to the past generations who steered Griffin Brewery over the years. Without the solid foundations which they laid, we would not be on such a sound financial footing as we are now, nor would we have progressed to the size and profitability we currently enjoy.

I am most grateful for the help we have received from the late Gillian Morris, who started researching for us, and her mother, Doris Yarde, who carried on after her daughter died and delved so deeply into our past to produce and collate all the details needed in order for the book to be produced.

ANTHONY FULLER CBE
Chairman  Fuller, Smith & Turner PLC

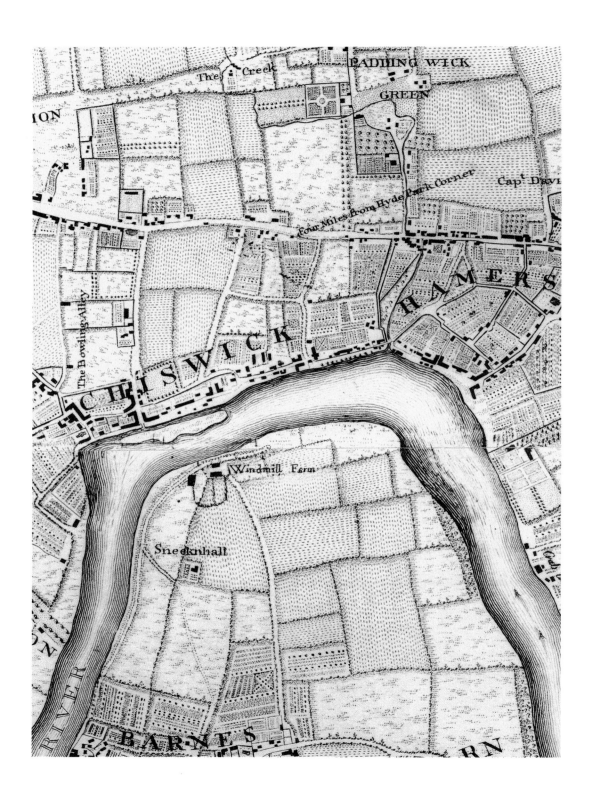

*Chapter 1*

# TWO BREWHOUSES
# ON THE MALL

ew monarchs have enjoyed beer quite as much as Elizabeth I. At breakfast, she drank a brew "so strong there was no man durst touch it". Whenever she set out on a summer expedition to extract hospitality from her courtiers in the shires, her baggage train always carried a good supply of this powerful stuff.

In 1602, the Queen was entertained by Sir William Russell at Corney House, on the banks of the Thames in Chiswick. Did she have her own special ale for breakfast? Or was she tempted by the product of the nearby brewhouse on the Corney estate? In those days most large households still brewed their own beer, and consumed it in huge quantities. A lease dated 16 December 1588 records that one William Hudson had taken on "a Brew House, Horsemill and Chambers at Chiswick... for five years at 40/- per year". This belonged to Corney House.

We shall never know whether or not Queen Elizabeth actually did drink the local ale. All the

CORNEY HOUSE, CHISWICK, AS IT WAS IN 1760. A BREWHOUSE ON THE CORNEY ESTATE IN THE 16TH CENTURY MARKS THE BEGINNING OF THE BREWING INDUSTRY IN CHISWICK

(*LEFT*) MAP OF CHISWICK AND DISTRICT, 1747

same, the existence of the lease establishes a history of brewing in Chiswick since at least the year of the Spanish Armada. Corney House no longer stands, but it was roughly half a mile west of the present Griffin Brewery.

By this time, however, home-brewing was in decline. The old-fashioned "ale", made simply of water, yeast and malt, had been transformed into "beer" by the addition of hops during the fifteenth century. The hops not only added a delicious, and much needed, bitterness to the flavour: they also improved the keeping qualities of the brew. This encouraged the

{ 9 }

commercial, or common, brewers to expand their businesses and deliver further afield. As beer gradually overtook ale in popularity, so the common brewers began to replace the domestic brewers. By the early seventeenth century, even the publican-brewers were bowing to the might of the big producers.

Elizabeth's immediate successors do not seem to have shared her enthusiasm for beer. In 1614, James I imposed a tax on malt of fourpence a quarter. When the Civil War broke out in 1642, both Charles I and the Parliamentarians raised revenue for their rival armies by slapping duty on beer itself. Though intended as a temporary measure, this tax was not lifted until 1830. Despite it, the common brewers continued to grow at the expense of their smaller competitors.

By the time of the Restoration, there were at least two brewhouses in Chiswick. The Russell family was now living at Bedford House, which had been built for the Earl of Bedford at the west end of Chiswick Mall. A lease of January 1661 describes it as including a "dovehouse, brewhouse, orchard, pond and five gardens" and with "those two messuages adjoining being converted and made into a brewhouse and other necessary outhouses". This stood at the rear of Bedford House, with a passageway leading to Chiswick Lane. When Edward Russell died in 1665, the estate was sold to one Thomas Plukenett.

Meanwhile, a rather humbler concern was operating nearby, where Thomas Urlin and his wife lived in a modest cottage at the Mall end of Chiswick Lane. The Hearth Tax returns for 1671 state that Urlin had "3 hearths and one brew chimney". The latter was on land south of the passageway leading to Bedford House, with Chiswick Lane to the east and Brick Lane to the north. There is no way of telling whether or not Urlin throve. When he died in 1682 his business passed to his widow and son-in-law.

A key figure in the history of the Griffin Brewery now made his entrance. His name was Thomas Mawson, and he clearly had ambition. Arriving in Chiswick in the 1680s he proceeded, within two decades, to lay the foundations for a major brewing enterprise, beginning as manager for Mrs Urlin. By 1699 he had bought up Urlin's equipment and leased "one cottage, five tenements, two orchards and a garden" on the site. Expansion was rapid. Mawson soon purchased the George public house, now the George and Devonshire, and two adjoining cottages for £70. In 1701, he bought the Bedford House brewhouse from the Plukenetts, later uniting the two properties by acquiring the slip of land used as a passageway between them. The premises of the present brewery were beginning to take shape.

When Thomas Mawson died in 1714 at the age of 58, he was described as "a rich brewer". Just how rich may be judged from his Will. To his eldest son, Thomas, went the brewery (after his widow's death), including "malthouse, brewhouse, stables and outhouses together with malting utensils, coppers, backs and tunns and other utensils". To his second son Matthias he left his estate in the manor of Sutton Court and a freehold house in Chiswick. His third son Benjamin received land in Acton, four houses on Turnham Green and two in Chiswick village, and his youngest son William, three houses and two barns in Chiswick, the King's Head, and land in Ealing.

In the event, Benjamin and William Mawson died young, whilst Matthias followed a distinguished career in the Church. So it was Thomas junior who carried on the brewing business alone; and when his energy, or enthusiasm, waned in 1740, he leased the premises to another local brewer, William Harvest of Brentford.

Thomas Mawson died in 1748, leaving his brewery interests to his brother Matthias (who was at this time Bishop of Chichester, and later became Bishop of Ely). Matthias had no working interest in the brewery, and it was now that another - and more dynamic - personality stepped in. Matthew Graves was an affluent solicitor of the Inner Temple, in search of a lucrative business venture in which to invest. He saw that the brewing industry was heading for a boom, and promptly took on the lease of Mawson's property (retaining Harvest as the brewer). The shrewd Graves also realized that selling beer was just as important as making it. He began leasing inns in the Chiswick area, paying £200 for the Coach and Horses on Turnham Green and going on to acquire, among others, the Red Lion at Acton, the Catherine Wheel at Brentford, the Bull's Head at Strand-on-the-Green and the Three Jolly Gardeners at Hammersmith. These were added to existing outlets for the brewery, owned or leased by the Mawson family, and including the Fox and Dogs in Chiswick and The Barge Aground at Brentford.

On the Bishop's death, the property was bequeathed to his niece. She in turn passed her interests on to her son, Charles Purvis. Graves continued to build up his estate. In 1777, he became tenant of

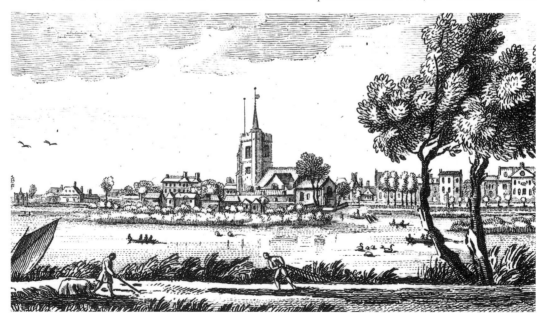

THE SOUTH VIEW OF CHISWICK, 1750. CORNEY HOUSE IS IMMEDIATELY TO THE LEFT OF ST NICHOLAS CHURCH, WITH BEDFORD HOUSE ON THE FAR RIGHT OF THE PICTURE

the Red Lion Inn and eight adjoining cottages in Chiswick Lane and Chiswick Mall. This was the last eighteenth-century acquisition, completing the eastern half of the present brewery premises.

The *Gentleman's Magazine* for 1780 records the death of Matthew Graves, brewer, at the age of 69. In his Will, Graves rather whimsically stipulated that the brewhouse should go on operating for a further two years "and no longer, and then I do order the same to be disposed of". Thus it came about in 1782 that the brewery, with its tangle of different freeholds and copyholds, was put on the market once again.

That autumn a "rest", or inventory, of the entire Graves estate was drawn up. It gives a vivid picture of the establishment and its hardware:

The Cooper's Shop: the cooper's tools; 500 Rivets; 200 Twopenny Nails; 1 Pewter Crane; 1 old bad Crane and 1 old Grindstone and Trough.

The Counting House: 1 Wainscoat Desk; 1 Iron Chest; 1 Poker, Shovel, Tongs and Grate; 1 Windsor Chair; ½ Pint Silver Pot; 1 Stool; 1 Pewter Ink Stand.

The Tun Room: Yeast Stands; 3 Copper Filing Kettles; 216 foot of Old Leather Pipe; 3 Brass Screws; 92 foot of Good Leather Pipe.

Uppon the Stage: Tubs and Hoops.

The Malt Loft: 2 Old Bushell Measures; 1 Malt Screen; 1 Plank; 1 Old Shovel.

The Yards: 9 old Stinking Butts unhead'd; 3 old Stinking Puncheons; 3 old Stinking Barrells; 1 Old Boar; 3 Old Sows; 2 Good Piggs; 10 Young Piggs.

The Coach House and Stable: 1 Puncheon Binn, Lock and Key; 1 Water Butt Tub.

Dray Horse Stable: Tubs and Hoops; 3 Dung Forks; 3 Old Shovels; a Parcel of Chalk.

The Stoker Room: 1 old Bed; 1 Blankett; 1 Quilt; 1 Table; 1 Chair.

Coopers' Lobby: Barrell Stands; 1 Hair Sieve; 1 Burning Iron; 1 Cork Basket.

Coopers' Room: 1 Old Binn; 2 Quart Copper Pots; 1 Gallon Vitriol; 36lbs Ising Glass.

Hop Loft: 2 Old Shovels; 1 Pair Scales with 4...56lbs, 2...28lbs, 2...14lbs, 2...7lbs, 2...2lbs, 1...1lb weights. 3 dozen and 6 Brooms; 3 old Ropes; 6 Coal Sacks.

Cash in Counting House... £998-0-0

Total Valuation of Brewhouse... £63-0-0

Entire valuation of the Estate... £10,273-12-8

This collection of barrels, livestock and leather piping hardly sounds like the basis for amassing a fortune. Yet the mundanity of the inventory is misleading: brewing was very big business. Only a year before, Thrale's Brewery in Southwark had been sold up, on the owner's death, for £135,000. Samuel Johnson, a close friend of the widow, had helped with the transaction, glorying in the unaccustomed role of entrepreneur. When asked the value of the property, he had loftily replied:

"We are not here to sell a parcel of boilers and vats, but the potentiality of growing rich beyond the dreams of avarice."

This utterance might have drawn a hollow laugh from the two prospective purchasers of the Chiswick breweries. John Thompson, a maltster, and David Roberts, a distiller, quickly found themselves knee-deep in a morass of litigation and conveyancing. Having agreed to pay the asking price of £10,273, they were confronted by unexpected demands from the Graves family. It appeared that George, Graves's son, would not reach his twenty-first birthday until 1787, and was therefore entitled to all the rents until then. Thompson and Roberts fought the claim. The case dragged through the Court of Chancery, where it was eventually settled in George's favour. The purchasers had to pay over an additional £5,746.

THESE CONTEMPORARY VIEWS OF AN 18TH-CENTURY LONDON BREWHOUSE SHOW A LABOUR-INTENSIVE INDUSTRY

Meanwhile, the solicitor acting for Thompson and Roberts was having great difficulty in drawing up a single conveyance from the mass of title deeds to the various other properties. He was not helped by the fact that the Mawson family vault stood on the land. There was much fretting lest the new owners should disturb the bones and coffins.

It is no real surprise to hear that David Roberts withdrew from the partnership in 1786, and relinquished his share; but his reason was not frustration. He had been appointed to the

Household of King George III at Kew Palace, where he was to teach the Queen and the Royal children drawing, English and handwriting. This forced him to renounce all connections with vulgar "Trade".

So John Thompson soldiered on alone, and for several years the brewery flourished. Catastrophe, however, was not far away. Although Thompson himself appears to have been a man of the utmost probity, there was a shady element in his wife's family which was to bring the business close to ruin. The first hint of this had come in an apparently irrelevant episode in 1780, when Captain Henry Bryne (Thompson's brother-in-law) had been lost at sea in a hurricane. Thompson began to sort out Bryne's affairs. He was astonished to discover that the late captain had been a highly organized smuggler of woollen goods, with a network of "ladies" in various trading ports who sold on his contraband. The strain of dishonesty was to surface in the next generation, most notably in Thompson's two sons - Douglas and Henry.

This pair took over the brewery when their father died in 1807. At first all went smoothly. Sales and production increased, and in 1816 the brothers bought Newton's Brewery and eleven public houses in Brentford, Isleworth and Norwood Green. They did this with the aid of a mortgage of

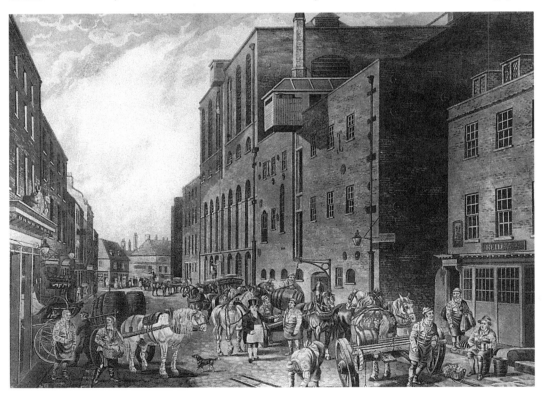

REID'S OLD GRIFFIN BREWERY IN CLERKENWELL, CIRCA 1820. THE GRIFFIN NAME WAS PURLOINED BY THE THOMPSON BROTHERS AND BECAME THE SYMBOL FOR THE CHISWICK BREWERY

£18,000 from one Thomas Harrington. That same year also saw the first appearance of the name "Griffin Brewery" in Chiswick. The Griffin had for several years been the symbol of Meux and Reid's Brewery in Liquorpond Street in the City. When that partnership broke up in rancorous circumstances, the beady Douglas snaffled the name, which has been retained ever since (though the Griffin trade mark was not officially granted until 1892).

Things began to go wrong in 1821. Douglas Thompson's first wife died, and shortly afterwards he married Hannah Hill. For this happy event, he had to provide a marriage settlement of £300 a year. But where was he to find it? Without blinking - and without telling his brother - Douglas took out another mortgage on all the brewery premises, this time for £6,000, over a period of five hundred years. The marriage was soon blessed with a son, though the boy was regarded as an imbecile. He was christened, ominously, with the family name of Bryne.

Henry, meanwhile, had also begun taking out extra mortgages in order to purchase or lease more public houses. Naturally, he neglected to inform Douglas.

By 1826, the Thompson brothers were in trouble. They must have defaulted on the main mortgage repayments to Thomas Harrington, for they were forced to surrender various copyholds to him. To their horror, Harrington and the other mortgagees discovered that many of the properties were worth much less than they had been told.

The brothers had claimed, for example, that the Black Horse at Greenford had been bought freehold. In fact, it was only copyhold, which made a considerable difference to its value. Henry and Douglas were given six months to extricate themselves from the sale: if not, they would be accused of fraud.

Needless to say, there was no money available for the refund. It had all been lost in other ventures. As the pressure mounted, the extent of Henry's double dealing was revealed. He had routinely pushed up the valuations of properties to ridiculous levels in order to get bigger mortgages. Now, he was unable to meet the repayment demands. Retribution and ruin stared the Thompsons in the face.

Yet somehow they stayed out of the courts; and somehow the brewery continued to survive. Indeed Henry, in a bitter letter to his brother, claimed that he alone had managed to increase sales from 8,000 barrels in 1807 to 24,000 barrels in 1828. The squabbling intensified, but the Thompsons still had enough cunning to search for a way out of their dire situation.

Money was needed, and plenty of it. They approached Philip Wood, a member of an old-established family of hop merchants, and brother of London's Lord Mayor, and invited him to become a partner. It did not take Wood long to realize that even his wealth was not enough to save the business. He, in his turn, approached a country gentleman in Wiltshire, and proposed that he too should enter the partnership. The gentleman's name was John Fuller.

*Chapter 2*

# EXIT THOMPSON, ENTER SMITH AND TURNER

**J**ohn Fuller was a fortunate man. Born in 1765, he had become the protégé of a wealthy distant cousin, a financier and moneylender named Gerrard Dutton Fleetwood. Indeed, John and his wife seem to have lived with Fleetwood in his home in Leatherhead. When Fleetwood died in 1795, Fuller inherited his entire fortune - and his "loan book". In 1801 he purchased the estate of Neston Park, near Corsham in Wiltshire, which has been the family seat ever since.

When Wood's offer of partnership arrived on the Neston Park breakfast table, Fuller was already an old man. But he rose to the challenge. Here was a fine opportunity to invest money on behalf of his son, John Bird Fuller.

CHISWICK MALL IN 1820. THIS PICTURESQUE PART OF THE RIVER STILL PROVIDES A TRANQUIL SETTING FOR THE BUSTLING ACTIVITY OF FULLER'S BREWERY

Fuller may also have recalled that the family already had one connection, albeit a tenuous one, with the Chiswick neighbourhood. This was the affable clergyman and historian Dr Thomas Fuller, who had been rector of the nearby village of Cranford between 1658 and 1661. Dr Fuller had a great reputation as a preacher, and a rather lesser one as the writer of innumerable poems, satires, pamphlets and histories. The best known of these was his *History of the Worthies of England*, a series of lives of notable Englishmen, which displays much wit and learning, as well as a lamentable fondness for puns. He even suggested his own epitaph: "Fuller's Earth". But perhaps the Doctor's most fitting memorial is the description of him by Charles Lamb as a "dear, fine, silly, old angel".

There was nothing silly about Thomas Fuller's descendant John. He seized the business opportunity offered by Wood and within a few years had stamped his authority on the affairs of the brewery, even though he rarely visited it. The original, equal, partnership of Thompson, Wood and Fuller, established in 1829, was a short-lived one. Henry Thompson sold his share in the company, squandered the capital and was declared a bankrupt in 1831. Philip Wood died in 1832 (and it soon became clear that he too had been bankrupt). Fuller bought his share, thus becoming the major shareholder, with two-thirds of the total.

The brewery's finances were still distinctly rocky, however. Beer sales had slumped in 1831, causing a loss of over £3,000 for the year. Even more worrying was the plight of Douglas, the remaining Thompson. He already owed the company £14,000, and was about to become liable for his brother's equally massive debts. Fuller now tightened his grip by allowing Douglas to borrow further from the business, using his third share as a mortgage.

On 5 January 1832, Fuller and Thompson signed their new articles of partnership, which were intended to last for eighteen years. This

COUNTRY GENTLEMAN JOHN FULLER, WHO CAME TO THE RESCUE OF THE BREWERY IN 1829 AND FOUNDED A BREWING DYNASTY, THOUGH NOT WITHOUT DIFFICULTY

proved to be hopelessly optimistic. The articles defined Douglas as "the resident and acting partner", who was to "devote the whole of his time and energy to the business" while John Fuller spent most of his time in Wiltshire. It was very soon clear that Douglas Thompson was not so much a partner as an albatross round Fuller's neck. Weak, feckless and muddle-headed, he seemed entirely under the thumb of his domineering second wife.

Fuller was well aware of Douglas's shortcomings. To safeguard his own interests, and to keep a close eye on affairs in Chiswick, he hired an accountant named J.W.Smith. Smith was to visit the brewery once a week and compile a report on purchases, sales and beer production which he would send down to Neston.

Smith was one of several characters haunting the Griffin Brewery during this period who might have walked straight out of the pages of Dickens. Through his reports, we gain a picture of a dour and humourless middle-aged man, devoted to his job and meticulous in his paperwork: in short, the very antithesis of Douglas Thompson. Smith was inordinately proud of his position as auditor to the Carlton, Athenaeum and Travellers' Clubs, and made regular appearances in the Chancery Courts.

The plunge into the scruffy, deceitful, extravagant world of the Thompson family must have pained him deeply.

Another Dickensian personality is known to us only by his surname of Slee, and he caused Smith even more trouble. Slee had originally been hired by Wood and Thompson to run a newly built Spirit Store at the brewery. Even by their standards, this was a bizarre step, for Slee was at the time in France, where he had fled to escape prosecution by the Excise. In his absence, his house in Brighton was searched, and "some most extraordinary contrivance for smuggling and cheating the Government" was found. A less suitable person to take charge of a spirit store it would be hard to imagine.

NESTON PARK, NEAR CORSHAM, SHORTLY AFTER JOHN FULLER PURCHASED THE ESTATE IN 1801. STILL THE FAMILY SEAT OF THE FULLERS, IT IS CURRENTLY THE HOME OF MAJOR SIR JOHN FULLER BT

Nevertheless, Slee in due course arrived at his new post. The tight-lipped Smith watched him closely and reported regularly to his employer. Slee, he disclosed, was in the habit of visiting public houses and making ridiculous promises about supplies to the tenants. Worse still, "his conduct at Chiswick has been most disreputable: he has seduced and has been living openly with one of Mr Thompson's maids, who was at last turned out of Slee's house by his own Daughter". He also gave jobs in the store to brothers of "the woman whom he had debauched". It is no surprise to read that by June 1834 the Spirit Store had been closed down and Slee dismissed. Even so, he managed to slip away with two dozen bottles of unsold wine from the cellar.

Exasperation with Thompson filled the letters which passed between John Fuller and J.W.Smith. "My opinion," wrote Fuller late in 1834, "is that the whole family possesses very much the same principles, that is they care not as to any matter of right whose property they get into their hands to lavish away. The Brewery business is going on flourishingly but we must not expect all sunshine and fair weather. I know the great risk and hazard I have taken on myself..."

Shortly after this, a fresh disaster hit Douglas Thompson. His eldest son had understandably turned his back on the family business and emigrated to Western Australia, where he had been granted an area of land. In 1835, he was drowned when his moth-eaten boat sank in the Swan River - an echo of the fate of old Captain Bryne. Douglas only heard of the tragedy in 1836, when he read about it in a newspaper. Pausing briefly to wipe away a tear, he dashed off a begging letter to the Governor in Perth, claiming his son's land. The lad, he said, "had received from me altogether £15 to £1700. A sum which then I could ill spare owing to the unfortunate circumstances in which I had been placed by the ill-management of his uncle... Upon the winding up of the concern I found myself the loser to the amount of at least £20,000. In fact I am absolutely beginning again."

Douglas was obviously just as great a humbug as his brother. One is glad to note that, despite several years of campaigning, the claim came to nothing.

In March 1839, John Fuller died aged 74 after a severe attack of influenza. His estates, and his problems, were inherited by his son, John Bird Fuller. Brewery profits were falling sharply. This was the beginning of the "Hungry Forties", when many poor people could scarcely afford bread, let alone beer.

But the most immediate concern was Douglas Thompson who had, with unfaltering imprudence, landed the brewery in a fresh crisis. His shrewish second wife died, and he hastily married for a third time. The object of his affection on this occasion was a widow with no fewer than seven children. "She is," noted Smith with alarm, "the daughter of our maltster, Muggeridge", and the match was "a result of a deep-laid scheme to supply the brewery with malt and hops as the sole supplier."

This was really shocking news. Under the existing deed of partnership, provision had to be made for all Douglas Thompson's dependants in the event of his death. The number of dependants had now swollen to over a dozen, including the imbecile Bryne. Such a liability, added to Douglas's still outstanding debts, was too much to bear.

John Bird Fuller moved swiftly. In January 1841 he informed Douglas that their partnership was to be dissolved within twelve months. The faithful J.W.Smith would become manager in his place. If Douglas relinquished his share in the business, he would be paid an allowance of £400 a year. These were pretty generous terms, but Thompson squealed loudly that no provision had been made for his large family. Fuller was not to be distracted. He tightened the screw by withdrawing Thompson's right to draw cheques. This forced surrender, and the Deed of Dissolution took effect from January 1842.

However, it was not that easy to get rid of the Thompson family altogether. The disgraced Henry made a pathetic reappearance, offering his services as manager, and blaming his past disasters on his brother and Philip Wood. It was his last gasp, for he died a month later. Douglas, meanwhile, had been evicted from the brewery and had fled to Calais, leaving his family and finances in chaos behind him. Showing extraordinary patience, Fuller arranged support for the wife and children (even the wretched Bryne was granted £5 a quarter). Gradually, the Thompson nightmare faded.

A great deal of salvage work remained to be done. Fuller had to convince the brewing industry, and the business world at large, that for the first time in thirty-five years an honest man was in control of the Chiswick premises. Aided by the punctilious J.W.Smith, he began to restore the brewery's reputation. How gratified Smith must have been when the company received a glowing letter from William Gutteridge, a local

THE THREE ORIGINAL PARTNERS IN FULLER, SMITH AND TURNER: (*L TO R*) JOHN BIRD FULLER WHO INHERITED HIS FATHER'S INTEREST IN THE BREWERY; HENRY SMITH, WHO JOINED HIM FROM THE ROMFORD BREWERY OF IND & SMITH; AND JOHN TURNER, BROTHER-IN-LAW OF HENRY AND HEAD BREWER AT ROMFORD

estate agent. Gutteridge wrote: "The Gentlemanly and Businesslike manner in which you appear as manager of the Chiswick Brewery not only reminds me of old times, but also in my idea reflects great credit upon the Principal of that Establishment, particularly after the treatment I have experienced from the original name."

Despite this encouragement, John Bird Fuller quickly recognized that his own resources were not enough to bring the brewery back to full health. He therefore cast about for new investors. His eye lit on John Smith (not to be confused with J.W.Smith), a wealthy partner of Edward Ind at the highly successful Romford Brewery. Somehow, Fuller persuaded John Smith to sever his ties with Ind and transfer his money from Romford to Chiswick in 1845. This move, incidentally, did no harm to Ind's career: he was joined by the brothers Coope and began trading under the name of Ind and

Coope. An agreement was made between the two ex-partners: Ind Coope would only trade to the east of the Aldgate Pump, and Fuller's to the west.

John Smith did not arrive alone. His investment in Fuller's brewery was made in the names of his son Henry Smith and son-in-law John Turner. Thus, for the first time, the three families were to be linked.

The actual process of drawing up the Articles of Partnership was to prove agonizingly slow. This was largely the fault of the ageing and slothful lawyer employed for the job, a Mr Frere of

THE ARTICLES OF PARTNERSHIP WERE SIGNED BY MESSRS FULLER, SMITH AND TURNER ON 19 NOVEMBER 1846

Lincoln's Inn. Frere's snail-like progress infuriated Fuller, who hated what he called "dilly-dallying". By August 1845 things had scarcely moved. John Smith visited his namesake at Chiswick and expressed concern at the continuing delay, which he warned could lose the brewery at least £1,000 a year in trade. J.W.Smith passed on this warning to Frere, and suggested an immediate meeting, at which matters might be hurried along. This was much too hasty for Mr Frere, who replied by messenger that he "would not be in Town for a few days".

The uncertainty heightened the tension between the prospective partners. Henry Smith, though only in his early thirties, was proving to be just as tough and determined a bargainer as John Bird Fuller. When Fuller declared that he must be allowed to appoint an agent to look after his affairs at the brewery, Smith objected very strongly. When the more easygoing John Turner mildly complained at the delay in letting him occupy the brewer's house, Smith argued his case. Smith's father, meanwhile, was losing enthusiasm for the affair and threatening to withdraw his money.

At the centre of these increasingly testy exchanges was poor J.W.Smith. Already alarmed at the prospect of being deprived of his old position, he now had to act as go-between for the warring factions, without provoking John Smith or J.B.Fuller. One has to admire Smith's delicate balancing act. He succeeds simultaneously in flattering his employer, encouraging Smith and Turner, badgering the lethargic Frere and fighting to keep his own place. "Messrs Smith and Turner have both declared that they do not see how they can get on without my assistance," he wrote to Frere. "It cannot be expected that while I have any connexion with the Brewery I should be content to sink into insignificance."

The New Year dawned, but Frere was still deaf to all exhortation. Indeed, he took to his bed with gout and bronchitis, followed by a long period of convalescence. As the months passed, a grim silence fell upon the parties concerned, and it was only by pleading old age that John Smith was at last able to goad the solicitor into action. The Articles of Partnership were signed on 19 November 1846.

Under the deed, Fuller retained one half of the total shares in the company, whilst Henry Smith and John Turner took one quarter each. For this they paid £31,000. They were termed "active resident partners", occupying "the manager's house and the outbuildings and gardens thereto situate at Chiswick except ONE room", which was to be reserved for Fuller's use. J.W.Smith, as he had feared, ceased to be manager but was retained as an accountant: his salary dropped from £700 to £300 as a result.

Henry Smith and John Turner brought with them a welcome bonus in the shape of an extensive list of private customers. For these, a special type of beer had to be brewed. It was known as "Table Beer", or HK (the "H" indicating that it was well hopped, and the "K" that it was a long-keeping beer). A mild version of this, called XK, was also on offer.

This was quite a change for the Griffin Brewery, which seems to have been remarkably conservative in its range of beers until then. Under the Thompsons, only two kinds had ever been brewed - ale, which sold at 54 shillings a barrel, and hock, at 33 shillings. Porter, which had soared in popularity since the 1740s, had not originally been produced on the premises, but bought in from other brewers. It was only in 1841 that porter brewing began at the Griffin - just when it was going into terminal decline as a national drink.

The arrival of John Turner certainly gave a much-needed lift to the technical side of the business. Old Thomas Marlow, the reliable and efficient head brewer, had died in 1845, and his replacement had turned out to be a bungler. John Bird Fuller, of course, knew absolutely nothing about the brewing process, and must have been mightily relieved when Turner took over. In 1850 Turner's son John E.Turner, known for short as John Junior, came of age and was appointed head brewer at a salary of £100 a year. He held this position until his death in 1884, but never became a partner.

Now, at last, the fortunes of the brewery entered calmer waters. One of the later Fullers, Dillwyn Fleetwood, made a series of notes on this period. He wrote:

During all these years the business continued to flourish; taxation was light, there was no beer duty. Employment, in the neighbourhood at any rate, was good; therefore there was plenty of money to spend on beer, which was both strong and cheap. Whether it was also uniformly good is rather more than doubtful. However that may have been, the Private Trade, after making a modest start in 1846 with 3,433 barrels and gross receipts of £4,298 (while the gross receipts from the Publican Trade were £40,570), increased steadily until in 1866 it shows gross receipts of £46,081 against the Public Trade's £45,543.

The new dynasty of Fuller, Smith and Turner had clearly brought stability, and profitability, to the sign of the Griffin.

# Chapter 3

# DISAGREEMENTS AND DEVELOPMENTS

**F**uller, Smith and Turner now had all the appearance of being a comfortable family firm. But, as with all family firms, it had one incurably weak link - the question of succession. Partners grew old or died; their successors were nominated; some were assets to the company; some were most definitely not; and some were simply not interested. This uncertainty preyed on the minds of the three families, periodically erupting into squabbles over the next half-century.

The first of these disputes bubbled up as early as 1851. Henry Smith, though heading into middle age, was still a bachelor living with the Turners at the Brewery House. Now it emerged that he was having "an affair with his fancy", as one of the partners put it, and his fancy had a disgruntled husband.

Though essentially a private matter, this revelation was the cause of great consternation at the brewery. John Smith, every inch the stern Victorian father, expressed his outrage by threatening to withdraw his money (and thus Henry's quarter share) from the business. John Turner sprang to Smith's defence with some characteristically blunt language. The only one left to make peace was John Bird Fuller. He summoned Henry Smith to Neston and persuaded him to write two letters: one to the lady, ending the liaison, and the other to his father, offering an apology. "I can scarcely think," Fuller confided to his accountant, "Mr John Smith intends to take such strong measures of withdrawing his money, throwing as it were his son out of bread . . . "

But John Smith was hard to mollify. He would not be swayed by the pleadings of his partners or his son. The future of the enterprise looked bleak. With heavy heart, Fuller prepared to dissolve the partnership and buy out Henry's share himself.

Here, tantalizingly, the episode ends. History does not relate the climax to this scandal - only the aftermath. Evidently, Smith relented, forgave his son and continued with the original arrangement, for everything went on as before. Indeed, Henry seems to have turned into a model citizen in later years (though he never married), being a prominent benefactor of St Nicholas Church. He also served as a Chiswick Improvement Commissioner from 1858. This body of worthy men, which included John Turner, was responsible for overseeing the upkeep of the local sewers, drains

and roads, and for maintaining a wharf on the Thames. Chiswick had grown rapidly, doubling its population between 1841 and 1861, and such things had become vital to the health of the area.

John Bird Fuller was now looking to the future with confidence. There was, at any rate, no problem about who was to succeed him. His eldest son, John Augustus, was serving with the British Army in the Crimean War, but fully intended to take on his father's role at the brewery in due course. His second son, George Pargiter, had just finished at Oxford. "There are not to be found two more prudent and well disposed young men," wrote Fuller proudly.

During 1856 there appeared in Fuller's private ledger the entry "J.W.Smith died - regrettable". Rarely can so faithful a servant have been given so offhanded an epitaph.

A link with the past had thus been broken; and, within a few years, a link with the future had tragically gone too. John Augustus had remained in the army, and was by 1859 stationed on

*CHISWICK FROM THE RIVER, A PAINTING BY JACOB KNYFF (C.1675) SHOWING ST NICHOLAS CHURCH. HENRY SMITH WAS A BENEFACTOR WHEN THE CHURCH WAS RESTORED IN THE 19TH CENTURY, AND IN 1924 THE FUNERAL OF MAJOR R F L TURNER TOOK PLACE THERE. JOHN TURNER AND 'TREVY' TURNER ARE ALSO BURIED AT ST NICHOLAS*

Gibraltar. News was scarce, but as far as the family knew he had either been wounded or had fallen ill. In September of that year, John Bird Fuller received the last letter he was ever to get from his eldest son:

> This morning I brought up a good quantity of blood from my chest and I now begin to think it possible that my present illness may turn out fatal ... I wish it had been permitted me to see dear old Neston once more and I am afraid the news of my death will come upon you all with dreadful suddenness.

By the time John Bird read these words, John Augustus was already dead. In his grief, the old man turned to pin all his hopes on his other son, George Pargiter. Now was the moment for him to begin his training at the brewery (he had been drawing a salary of £150 a year since 1856) and prepare to take command.

Meanwhile business continued to expand, and a considerable amount of building was done. Between 1855 and 1863, a new stores and two new tun rooms were completed. Turnover rose nicely and, with the expiration of the first Deed of Partnership looming in 1866, Smith and Turner began pressing Fuller for a bigger slice of the cake. They pointed out that, since they had arrived, the average annual profits had risen from just over £6,000 to more than £16,000. Nearly all the outstanding mortgages had been paid off, and many new properties had been purchased. In view of this, they demanded that they should be made co-equal partners with Fuller, each owning a third share.

John Bird refused even to entertain the idea. He tersely told Smith and Turner that they could either renew the existing terms of the partnership or be bought out. His only compromise was to offer the pair an increase in their salaries for managing the brewery.

The three men had once again reached what Fuller called a "deplorable deadlock". The only way out of it was to ask for an independent opinion from a barrister. Counsel George Markham Gifford pondered on the conflicting claims and solemnly declared that, if the parties could not concur, the whole brewery would have to be sold by private auction to the highest bidder. This bombshell must have brought everyone to their senses. As usual after such corporate crises there is no surviving correspondence, but Fuller, Smith and Turner seem to have patched up their differences for on 1 May 1866 they all signed the new Deed of Partnership. The proportion of the shares - and most other clauses - remained as before. The one vital alteration was that Smith and Turner were to be paid a percentage commission on sales to the private trade. Presumably this satisfied them.

Another period of comparative tranquillity followed this storm. The company ledgers give a picture of steady growth and improvement. During 1866, a new store and tun room, a new stable and a store beneath the garden were built. The brewery owned over £12,000 worth of "Cooperage, Firkins and

Kilderfirkins". This was a sure sign of a healthy trading position, as was the "Horses Account" of £4,901, which showed a stock of thirty-six horses. These more than earned their keep, not only by hard work but also by producing manure which was sold for £45 per cartload. In summer, they grazed in the adjoining "Home fields", alongside the pens where the brewery's pigs grew fat on spent barley.

Chiswick was, even at this stage, a relatively peaceful community, beyond the bounds of Hammersmith. But it was beginning to expand rapidly. The brewery itself was in what was now called Old Chiswick. There was a growing residential area along the Mall, with smaller properties going up around Chiswick Lane and Devonshire Road. The Rate Books show that many brewery employees lived in the vicinity, though not all of them worked for Fuller, Smith and Turner. The Griffin Brewery had a close rival right on its doorstep. This was the Lamb Brewery,

# £100 REWARD.
# ABSCONDED
On 12th inst., from the service of Messrs. Fuller, Smith, and Turner, Brewers, Chiswick, charged on warrant with embezzling £1,356.

# Thomas Humphreys,
the Collector. Age 40, height 5ft. 11 inches. complexion fresh, hair brown, eyes light, rather stout, little or no whisker, stoops when walking: supposed dark brown frock coat and vest, black cloth trousers, side spring boots, black hat, carried a light summer overcoat, and black glazed bag.

A Reward of £50 will be paid to any person giving such information as shall lead to the apprehension of the said Thomas Humphreys. And a further Reward of £50 on recovery of the money, or in proportion thereof.

Information to be given to Sergeant Clarke, Detective Office, Great Scotland Yard, or to any Police Station.

A RARE INSTANCE OF THEFT FROM THE BREWERY, SEPTEMBER 1867. AS FAR AS IS KNOWN, HE WAS NEVER APPREHENDED

owned by the Sich family and boasting, for many years, as big a workforce as its neighbour's.

On 27 May 1872, John Bird Fuller died. For nearly forty years, this honest, courteous and unyielding man had held the company together. Now he was to be succeeded by an altogether larger and more imaginative personality - his son George Pargiter Fuller, who inherited his half share.

George Pargiter (or GP, as he is still affectionately known by his descendants) is the most

NESTON. S. VIEW.

NESTON. W. VIEW.

formidable figure in the history of Fuller's, gripping the helm for over half a century. He is also one of the most interesting. As a brewery owner, he encouraged several new enterprises, such as the maltings, and sanctioned the latest technology and processes. As a farmer, he eagerly embraced modern methods, buying one of the earliest steam-powered hay driers and building his own automatic stock feeder, which was controlled by the mechanism from a grandfather clock! As a major landowner, he considerably expanded the house at Neston Park, and installed an electric generator and windmills for raising water. As a public figure, he was stoutly Liberal, serving as MP for Westbury from 1885 to 1895, and is reputed to have turned down a peerage. As a family man, he ensured a solid future by fathering five sons (and mapping out their careers) and a daughter.

GEORGE PARGITER FULLER, WHO HEADED THE COMPANY FOR MORE THAN 50 YEARS. A MAN OF GREAT ENTERPRISE AND VISION, HE ENCOURAGED MODERNIZATION AT BOTH THE BREWERY AND NESTON, AND AS A LIBERAL MP STOOD FOR REFORM

(LEFT) GEORGE PARGITER FULLER AND HIS WIFE EMILY AT NESTON, 1896. GP EXTENDED THE HOUSE, ADDING A PORTICO, CONSERVATORY AND BILLIARD ROOM. HE ALSO INSTALLED ELECTRICITY AT THE PROPERTY

GP's long reign began serenely enough. Indeed, the records contain no major crises - even with the signing of the third Deed of Partnership in 1887. For this portentous event, a fresh Inventory and Valuation was drawn up. It is an illuminating document, especially when compared with the "Rest" prepared a century earlier (see page 12). Here are some extracts describing the brewery premises:

On the right of the Entrance Yard, the Counting House, Strong Room and Offices. The private
Residence occupied by Mr Henry Smith. A building of three floors adjoining. Ground Floor
forming Kitchen etc, with Hop and Sugar Stores over - the Roof formed by the iron Cold
Liquor Back.

The Brewhouse, in which are the Mash Tuns, Coppers and other brewing plants.

The Malt Loft and Cellar under. Working Tun Rooms and Cleansing Rooms with Carpenters'
Shop and store rooms over one Beer Store.

Engine House, Boiler House, Vat House.

Timekeeper's Office and Allowance Store.

Settling Back Room and Fining Store.

Another Boiler House. Cask Shed.

Cask Steaming Shed with Boiler and Engine House at the end.

A large Stable Yard (partly paved) on three sides of which are the following stables etc. 20 Stall
Stables with Loft and Corn Store over.

Stable for 30 horses.

Also Stall Nag Stable with Harness Room, Coach House and 2 loose boxes.

A Smithy and Cooperage. Another 4 stall stables with man's room adjoining.

On the left hand side of the Entrance Yard opposite the Offices and Residences are the Loading
Out Store and Four Beer Stores with vaulted Cellar below and a Garden with vaulted Beer
Store under. The Site with Wells and Yard etc.


The greater part of all this was owned freehold. Much of the remainder was held on a ninety-
nine-year lease at an annual rent of £60.

The third Deed of Partnership was duly signed on 19 July 1887. John Turner had already decided
to retire, so the new agreement was between G.P.Fuller and Henry Smith, plus GP's son William
Fleetwood and Henry's nephew Frank Smith. But this combination was short-lived. Henry Smith
died five months later, and John Turner in the following autumn. Smith's share went to his nephew
Frank and his great-nephew Edward Trevelyan Turner, while Turner's went to his son by his second
marriage, Robert Frederick Lewis. Though all this was arranged amicably enough, it is clear that the
great problem of the succession was getting knottier with each year that passed.

This was soon to be vividly demonstrated by an episode which, starting as a minor annoyance,
was whipped up into yet another constitutional storm. It concerned the young Edward Trevelyan
Turner - Trevy to his family and to posterity. The son of J.E.Turner and grandson of old John
Turner, he grew up under a doting mother into an improvident and selfish youth. No sooner had
he become a very junior partner than he began requesting sums of money from the fund invested

THE DOVE (FORMERLY THE DOVES), HAMMERSMITH MALL, SKETCHED BY BERNARD DOVE. A PUB FOR OVER 500 YEARS, IT WAS

THE HAUNT OF WRITERS LIKE POPE, ADDISON AND STEELE, AND ARTISTS SUCH AS TURNER AND WILLIAM MORRIS

in his name. These grew from £100 in 1891 to £2,000 a year later.

In December 1893 the partners were flabbergasted to receive a demand from Trevy that he should be allowed to retire from the business after only seven years. This was not just unprecedented: it was an affront to the spirit of the brewery. However, once they had recovered from the shock, they realized that the loss would not be a great one. Trevy's resignation was accepted and made official with great alacrity.

Too late, Trevy saw the rashness of his action. He wrote to the partners explaining that his mother had "kicked up a bit" at his leaving the brewery, and withdrawing his original request. His pleading was in vain. So were his various court actions against the partners: they were adamant in not wanting him back, and the law was on their side. By mid-1894 Trevy accepted defeat, and made off with a good deal of umbrage - and his great-uncle's investment of £10,000.

THE NEXT GENERATION: EDWARD TREVELYAN TURNER, FRANK SMITH AND WILLIAM FULLER, 1887. ALL THREE WENT INTO THE BUSINESS, THOUGH IN THE CASE OF THE BOWLER-HATTED 'TREVY' TURNER, NOT FOR LONG

*Chapter 4*

# INTO THE TWENTIETH CENTURY

T he British brewing industry was undergoing a volcanic change. In 1870, there had been 133,840 licensed brewers in England and Wales. By 1894, the total had crashed to 9,664. It was mostly the small-scale or pub brewers who had gone out of business, unable to compete with the mechanized plants, bulk prices and greater reliability of the big firms. Some of the very largest were floated as public companies, giving them even greater financial strength. There was a ferocious battle for outlets. The value of public houses doubled or, in some cases, trebled as their availability declined. In London, nearly all pubs had become "tied" houses by the end of the century.

GRIFFIN BREWERY CC AT HOMEFIELDS, 1886. FRANK SMITH (BOWLER HAT) IS SECOND FROM THE RIGHT IN THE BACK ROW.

WILLIAM FULLER IS IN THE CENTRE OF THE MIDDLE ROW, WITH 'TREVY' TURNER (STRIPED TIE) AND R F L TURNER ON HIS LEFT

So intense was the struggle that even some big brewers fell by the wayside. Others were forced to amalgamate (Mitchell's, for example, merging with Butler's in 1898).

Yet Fuller, Smith and Turner continued to thrive. This was partly due to more thoughtful marketing methods, beginning with a patent on the name "Griffin". The title had been unofficially purloined by Douglas Thompson many years before, and now a Mr T.P.Griffin objected to the brewery's unrestricted use of it. This meant a mountain of correspondence with the Board of Trade and the solicitors acting for both parties. In 1892 the matter was at last agreed, and the trade mark of the Griffin Brewery officially came into existence.

THE GRIFFIN BREWERY AS VIEWED FROM THE RIVER, 1890

Another, and much less troublesome, advertising ploy was the Fuller's balloon. It had been bought by William Fuller (GP's second son) in 1889, and emblazoned with the legend FULLER'S BEERS OF HONEST REPUTE in six-foot-high lettering. The balloon was flown for several years at Yarmouth Agricultural Show, at Windsor Races and at Kew or Hampton Court on Bank Holidays. At other times it floated majestically over the brewery premises.

In November 1896, the brewery achieved something of a publicity coup by being featured in the magazine *Pictorial Review*. This periodical called itself a "Compendium of Literature, Art, Fashion and Business Progress", under which latter heading fell the article on Fuller's. It is a tiresomely wordy and pompous piece, but nonetheless gives a detailed description of work at the Griffin Brewery.

The article opens with the arrival of the malt from the maltster's, which is then "conveyed to the top of the building by means of a Jacob's ladder, or endless band, of the shape only infinitely smaller of those we see used for dredging operations. The ladder travels through a closed shaft, discharging the malt into a hopper or receiver on the top floor. The malt here passes through revolving brushes, by which it is thoroughly cleaned. Then over a sieve, fitted with magnets for attracting any particles of metal that might injure the steel rollers, through which it subsequently passes, and is ground."

The writer was also struck by the device used for cooling the wort. "It is passed over refrigerators, and as this is a very ingenious apparatus . . . we will give a few words apropos. The refrigerators in question are a phalanx of metal tubes, presenting in appearance a Brobdingnagian washing board, on the ribs of which the maid rubs the clothes on washing day . . . Through the inside of these tubes cold water is continually running, and over the outer surface the wort moves in a thin sheet, extended over the whole mass of tubes." To keep out impurities, these refrigerators are "contained in an air-tight glass case, hermetically sealed."

The article contains several other intriguing sidelights. There is the description of the gloomy store where the old ale is kept in "immense vats" to mature - some of it for over a year. There is the list of aristocratic households to which Fuller's beer is supplied: this includes the Prince of Wales (later King Edward VII), the Duke of Edinburgh, Princess Victoria

(daughter of the old Queen), the Duke of Norfolk and the Duke of Marlborough. And there is mention of the brewery's water, "drawn from a well over 400 feet deep, the water from London chalk being gifted with unique brewing properties".

The unnamed author of the *Pictorial Review*'s article painted a portrait of a gleaming, hyper-efficient, germ-free plant, producing faultless beer. This, unfortunately, was not a true picture. During the 1890s, the brewery received a growing number of complaints about the quality of Fuller's products, some of which were going off far too quickly in store. George Pargiter was also getting

worried by the amount of material wasted in brewing and delivering. Far too great a percentage was being lost, he maintained in a letter: why, when he made jam at home, he allowed for only three per cent wastage during boiling!

It seems clear that, whilst the brewery's plant had grown more sophisticated, the brewer's techniques had lagged behind. Expert scientific advice was needed. This came in the shape of Doctor Edward Ralph Moritz, an analytical chemist of German extraction. He specialized in the chemistry of brewing, and in 1886 had been appointed as consultant to the Country Brewers' Society.

Shrewd, ambitious and formidably expert, he was to have a considerable effect on the company's fortunes. His arrival brings with it a thoroughly twentieth-century aura of white coats, test tubes and stainless steel - a piquant contrast to the cosy, wood-panelled, Victorian world of the partners.

Dr Moritz was asked to investigate the matter of the wastage. His report was prompt. The plant, he said, was not in a satisfactory state. He offered to make a more detailed investigation, recommend the necessary alterations, and personally supervise the carrying out of those recommendations. His fee for this would be £525. He further suggested that afterwards he should be retained as an independent consultant. There was obviously nothing diffident about Dr Moritz.

The partners were impressed by Moritz's style. When he estimated that the necessary improvements to the brewery would cost £6,500, no one protested - at least publicly. In private, they worried about the reaction of the incumbent head brewer, John Storey. Would he take offense at the open criticism of his work and at the interference of an outsider? At any rate, in June 1900 an agreement was signed, retaining the services of Dr Moritz for a period of twenty years.

The galvanic doctor wasted no time in bringing modern science to bear on the deteriorating quality of the "Griffin Brew". The main trouble was the poor standard of the malt, which was causing brews to "go off". Moritz's solution was simple, if daunting: the firm must manufacture its own malt, building a brand-new maltings for the purpose.

When the partners had regained their breath, they discussed the matter, and eventually gave their consent to this bold scheme. Hesitantly, they approached the Duke of Devonshire's agent and enquired the price of a stretch of land at Duke's Meadows. It was £1,500. By November 1900, the land had been purchased and proposals for the maltings buildings had been drawn up. Various builders were invited to tender for the contract.

The arrival of the tenders gave another, nastier shock. The builders' estimates varied between £33,000 and £39,000 exclusive of machinery, which would take the total cost to well over £40,000.

DELIVERING FULLER'S BEER AT THE TURN OF THE CENTURY. AT THIS TIME FULLER'S HAD SOME 8-10 DEPOTS ACROSS SOUTHERN ENGLAND, FROM SOUTH WALES TO EAST ANGLIA. BEER WAS DELIVERED TO THE DEPOTS BY TRAIN, THEN DISTRIBUTED LOCALLY BY HORSE-DRAWN VEHICLE OR HANDCART

George Pargiter would not countenance such expenditure. He instructed Dr Moritz to meet the architect and try to get the costs down. At the next partners' meeting, Moritz presented a revised estimate of £23,550. But GP was still not satisfied. Finally, in April 1902, a building contract was signed for £18,430, the work to be completed within forty-two weeks.

This was the beginning of a fresh nightmare for the partners. As building work began, and demands for expenses rose, they must have feared that Dr Moritz's dynamism had driven them along too fast. Here they were, saddled with a complex new enterprise which was soaking up

their working capital and forcing them to raise a new mortgage. At the same time, there were other financial worries. They had become liable for the debts of their hotel at Drayton Court (making yet another mortgage necessary), and the beginnings of a national recession had caused a slump in beer sales.

George Pargiter was something of an amateur statistician, and a compulsive scribbler of notes. Now he sat in his study at Neston Park, feverishly juggling with percentages and calculations which were aimed at making economies in the various brewery departments. His main concern had been to launch his five sons on suitable careers, and for these they needed stable incomes from the brewery.

John, the eldest, was already a successful politician, and was to be Liberal MP for Westbury between 1900 and 1911 before being appointed Governor of the Australian state of Victoria. William and Henry had been working as managers at the Griffin since the 1890s, although William was much more interested in hunting and cricket than brewing. He kept a pack of beagles next to the bottling store, and it was the delight of employees to lure the dogs into the store and get them drunk. Robert had bought a rubber company in Wiltshire (later to become Avon Rubber), whilst Edward, the youngest, had been established on the plantation of the Abbotsleigh Tea Company in Ceylon.

The brothers depended, to differing extents, upon the good health of the brewery. They each had ideas for helping the business out of its present crisis, and communicated them to each other in a good-natured way. After one encouraging letter from his eldest brother, Henry wrote back, "any appreciation of one's endeavour to put the business on a sound footing is most pleasant to a sensitive ass like me!" However, when the suggestion was made that the business should be turned into a limited company, both John and his father quickly squashed it.

Meanwhile, the effervescent Dr Moritz was dreaming up his own schemes for reviving profitability - though these, typically, involved the spending as well as the making of money. One was a duplication of existing plant which would, he insisted, save hops to the value of £1,000 a year. Another was a new wonder brew called "Protene Stout", which he had just invented. The partners were, as always, mesmerized by the doctor's enthusiasm, and not only bought the formula for the beer, but paid out extra money so that he could set up experimental equipment. However, after some initial excitement, "Protene Stout" disappeared from the agenda.

George Pargiter was now in his seventies, but his hold on the brewery reins was as firm as ever. When the expiration of the latest Deed of Partnership loomed in 1906, there was much heated talk about amalgamating with another brewery. GP was deeply upset. "This sweeping departure," he wrote, "from a policy carried out now for more than two generations, with what must be allowed to be extraordinary success and amity, positively alarmed me. I therefore felt bound to put in a veto... I am sure that you will feel when the time comes for providing occupation, remunerative as well as honourable, for the rising generation of the Fuller family, how valuable a family concern is to the happy fathers and mothers." These words have a peculiar resonance today, since Fuller's has survived - against all the commercial odds - as a "family concern".

Still, GP's defiance must have seemed unrealistic at the time. In 1906, the firm's debts stood at a staggering £220,000, with annual interest of 4.5 per cent. And yet another extra expense was being incurred. The original well had never provided enough water for the brewery, and had had to be supplemented from the mains. Over the next six years, engineers drilled away in an attempt to find a satisfactory new borehole. By 1912, they had reached a depth of 1,300 feet, but no water was found and the scheme was abandoned.

Apparently undeterred by this constant leaching of cash, the partners expanded their interests. In 1909, they purchased the Beehive Brewery, Brentford, which lay at the meeting of the backwaters of the Thames and the Grand Junction Canal. They did not need the brewery itself, which was sold off in lots. Their real gain was a total of thirty-four pubs, mostly free- or copyhold, which greatly increased the available outlets for Fuller's beers.

MAJOR ROBERT FREDERICK LEWIS TURNER, A PARTNER FOR OVER 30 YEARS AND CREATOR OF THE BREWERY'S ESTATE DEPARTMENT

At this point Dr Moritz surges back into the story with yet another bright idea. His latest project was something he called "The Secret Process". According to the minutes of the partners' meeting, he asked leave for "H.F.Fuller, Frank Smith and R.F.L.Turner to interest themselves in a syndicate for the manufacture of 'Extract of Malt'." Leave was granted, and for some months a furtive air surrounded the subject. Dr Moritz was busy applying for a patent and searching for a suitable name. This was more difficult than he imagined, and he began to lose patience. To the partners, he wrote: "You could call it 'The Starch

Dissolving Products Company', but that would give too much away. Call it what you like, I don't really care!" After some false starts, they settled on the professional title of "Solutal".

The new company began producing Solutal on brewery premises during 1911 using, one assumes, malt as the basic ingredient. Such was the need for secrecy that the exact nature of the product was not recorded anywhere, but it seems that a kind of starch was manufactured. This was sold to laundries in the area. Solutal had some initial success, but by 1915 the complaints were beginning to pour in. One laundry, in particular, pointed out that the stuff was discolouring their linen. A shortage of funds, made worse by the death of the wealthy Frank Smith in 1912, meant that no more research could be done. Solutal - though not, of course, Dr Moritz - slowly dropped out of sight.

The Great War of 1914-18 brought a whole new set of problems to the brewery. A growing number of employees (and partners) enlisted in the armed forces, leaving an acute shortage of labour. This forced upon the company the revolutionary step of employing women. By the end of the war, there were twenty-seven female labourers at work in the bottling and mineral water plants.

Beer sales fell drastically. This followed Lloyd George's declaration that "Drink is causing more damage in the war than all the German submarines put together", and the Defence of the Realm

THIS FULLER'S STAFF OUTING OF 1919 HAS A DISTINCTLY PATRIOTIC LOOK

Act, which limited pub opening hours. By 1917, matters had grown so serious that Fuller's signed an agreement to share resources with three nearby rivals - the Isleworth Brewery, the Lamb Brewery (Sich and Co) and the Victoria Brewery in Windsor.

This arrangement continued until the Armistice in November 1918, when the four went their separate ways again. But the Sich brothers never recovered their pre-war prosperity. In 1921, after protracted negotiations, they sold their premises and business to Watneys, who kept the valuable portfolio of pubs and sold the land and buildings on to Fuller, Smith and Turner for £23,400. Without the tied houses, the purchase was of limited value, although it gave room to expand the brewery slightly. Like a shadow of the past, the Sich's name can still be faintly seen on the wooden tower to the west of the present site.

THREE GENERATIONS OF CRICKETING FULLERS, ALL OF WHOM PLAYED FOR THE WINCHESTER COLLEGE XI AGAINST ETON. GEORGE PARGITER FULLER (*CENTRE*) PLAYED IN 1849-50 AND 51; H F FULLER (*RIGHT*) IN 1888; AND E H F FULLER IN 1921

# Chapter 5

# FULLER, SMITH & TURNER LIMITED

Gradually the old order changed. A Foden steam wagon puffed into the brewery, no doubt alarming the dray horses (an earlier trial of steam wagons had occurred at the turn of the century, with a locally built vehicle). It was on hire for a period of eight months from the Western Motor Transport Company. The cost, "@ £5 per day and overtime after 5 pm @ 10/- per hour", must have seemed fairly daunting. Yet, shortly afterwards, an order was given to Foden's London agents for "two 5 ton steam wagons costing £1,160 each with standard body - delivery in 3 months' time". Obviously they had proved their worth.

In 1922 Dillwyn Fuller, son of Henry Fleetwood, caused some astonishment by resigning his partnership in the company and joining Dr Moritz and his nephew in their consultancy. Intimate observers, however, would not have been surprised. Dillwyn had not enjoyed his life at the brewery:

A FODEN STEAM WAGON HERALDS THE END OF THE DRAY-HORSE ERA

relations with his father were often strained, and his departure was a relief to all. The doctor himself retired a few years later.

In 1924, Major Robert Frederick Lewis Turner, youngest son of John Turner, died at his home in Wimbledon. Called in as a very young man to help run the brewery, he had been a partner for over three decades and, among other things, had started up the Estate Department which built as well as maintained the various properties. His funeral at St Nicholas, Chiswick, was attended by the brewery staff and several tenants. The Last Post and Reveille were sounded over the grave by trumpeters of the Honourable Artillery Company.

HENRY FLEETWOOD FULLER, THE LAST SENIOR PARTNER, WHO BECAME THE FIRST CHAIRMAN OF FULLER, SMITH AND TURNER WHEN IT BECAME A PRIVATE LIMITED COMPANY IN 1929

The following year saw an intriguing departure from the unwritten law of the Fuller succession. Two new partners were admitted. One was Edward Hamilton Fleetwood Fuller, George Pargiter's grandson (and son of Edward the tea planter), who went on to become the first company secretary and second chairman. The other was Philip Stirling Eliot, prospective husband of Henry's daughter Joyce. Here was a conundrum. Henry obviously had his daughter's best interests at heart, but the admission of someone from outside the immediate family was not strictly permitted under the Articles of Partnership.

Once again, agitated letters flew between the partners. Once again, Counsel's opinion was called for. Once again, legal documents were drafted and re-drafted. Everybody insisted upon one immutable clause: that the share should remain with Joyce in the event of her fiancé's death. This would surely prevent any "outsiders" having a possible claim on the brewery. Henry Fuller wrote, "should there be no children to the marriage, I do not wish either party to have the power to appoint the share in business away from the Fuller family". Even now, the Thompson brothers were casting their appalling shadow. Happily, Eliot proved to be a tower of quiet, unassuming strength, and his extensive legal knowledge became invaluable.

The greatest change of all was heralded on 12 April 1927 in a simple sentence from the minutes: "The Partners have to report, with sincere regret, the death of Mr G.P.Fuller". George Pargiter had been born during the reign of William IV; he had been twelve years old when the partnership of

Fuller, Smith and Turner had first been formed, and for over half a century he had been the "father" of the partners, wielding enormous influence over the others. Though Liberal in politics, he had believed unbendingly in the traditional values of the partnership, and set his face against the invasive world of financial share-dealing.

With the passing of GP, the way at last lay open for Fuller, Smith and Turner to be registered as a private limited company. This was duly accomplished on 22 August 1929. It involved procedures of transfer which are standard at such moments, but still have a vague whisper of farce: one memorandum read, "An agreement for sale was entered into between Fuller, Smith and Turner and Fuller, Smith and Turner Ltd". However, there was nothing risible about the "consideration to be paid thereon", which was £1 million. The partners of the old firm, including William, Henry and Edward (Tony) Fuller, Alan Russell Smith, head brewer R.J.B.Storey and Philip Eliot, became the directors of the new, with their first meeting on 18 September. Henry Fuller was made chairman. The first share issue authorized 300,000 preference shares and 6,000 ordinary shares. The brewery had moved into a new and far more profitable era.

ALAN RUSSELL SMITH, FORMER PARTNER AND DIRECTOR. NEPHEW OF FRANK SMITH, HE WAS INVITED TO JOIN THE COMPANY WHEN HIS ELDEST BROTHER (HIS UNCLE'S ORIGINAL CHOICE) DIED PREMATURELY. HIS SON, JOHN RUSSELL SMITH, FOLLOWED HIM INTO THE BUSINESS, BECAME A DIRECTOR AND IS NOW VICE PRESIDENT OF FULLER'S

Meanwhile, another development was being planned which would have a massive, though less direct, influence on the future of Fuller's. This was the new Great West Road, which was intended to open up a fast route to the West, and bring relief to the old High Road in Chiswick. On the face of it, the brewery would be the loser. The new road would carve straight through the community, cutting off the Griffin premises and the old Chiswick river front from the rest of Chiswick. But it was to prove, in years to come, a blessing.

There was some immediate inconvenience when Middlesex County Council began issuing compulsory purchase orders to clear the way for digging. In 1928, the brewery was forced to sell a strip of land fronting Mawson Lane (part of the Lamb Brewery's garden). A year later, it lost the estate yard, van yard, carpenter's shop and cottages to the north of Mawson Lane.

The directors signed a new fourteen-year contract with Moritz and Partners at the start of 1930. The Moritz in question was not the Doctor, but his nephew Francis: one of his partners was, of course, Dillwyn Fuller. Dr Moritz had been long retired, and a few months later he died. There is no doubt that his expert advice and enthusiasm had transformed the quality of Fuller's beer since the late 1890s. During this time (according to the "appreciation" of Moritz in the Minute Book), the firm's profits had risen from £18,000 to £60,000. A glowing obituary in the *Institute of Brewing Journal* spoke of his "inspiring incentive to individualism".

One of Moritz's most successful legacies was the Maltings in Corney Road. From a doubtful and expensive beginning, it had grown into a thriving adjunct to the brewery, with increasing profits year by year. By the early 1930s, it was producing over 17,000 quarters of malt a year. In 1932, the Maltings became a private limited company, separate from the brewery. The parent company leased the site to Fuller's Maltings Limited for an annual rent of £500.

THE BOTTLING HALL AND

RACKING ROOM IN THE 1930s

But already the clouds of depression were gathering. In 1931 the Labour government had crumbled, unable to control the sliding economy. Among its less popular achievements was the raising of duty on beer from 80/- to 114/-, a measure which helped the national consumption of beer to fall from 24 million barrels to 18 million barrels a year.

Trade at the Griffin Brewery was badly hit. The dividend on ordinary shares for the nine months to 31 December 1932 fell to 5 per cent, and the directors were forced to take drastic measures. Wages were reduced by 10 per cent, and the brewery was shut down on Saturdays. It was not until the same period in 1934 that things returned to normal, and the ordinary shares dividend inched its way back to 11 per cent.

However, this state of normality was not to last for long. Fuller, Smith and Turner Limited was barely ten years old when Britain declared war on Germany in September 1939. Various emergency measures were quickly taken. The wine and spirit cellar was transformed into an air raid shelter for

up to eight hundred people: its roof was reinforced and bunks were fitted. Special leave of absence was granted for four of the directors (Philip Eliot, Edward and Christopher Fuller, and Lewis Turner) who had joined the armed forces. All four served throughout the war years and returned safely to the company. Scores of employees also joined up: by 1945, there were seventy-eight on active service.

The war soon reached the doorstep of the Griffin Brewery itself. On the night of 10 October 1940 German bombs hit the Maltings. The building was gutted by fire, and most of the plant and stock was destroyed. Elsewhere, an off-licence was demolished and over thirty pubs damaged. As the Blitz intensified, more and more properties suffered. In December another fire bomb attack damaged the brewery premises and destroyed more public houses.

Several of the employees worked as firewatchers during the bombing. One night, a fire bomb landed close to the Mawson Arms. It was soon dowsed with sand, and little damage was done. The firewatchers were officially commended for the quickness of their response to the incident. Nobody thought to point out that they had all been inside the Mawson Arms at the time.

Bombs, the black-out, shortage of labour and materials, an understandable slump in beer drinking - all these forced the directors into cutting back on production. In May 1941, the supply of bottled beer to on-licence houses and clubs was reduced by a third (later, cask beer was also rationed). By

FULLER'S CEASED MARKETING GINGER BEER AND LEMONADE AT THE OUTBREAK OF WORLD WAR II, BUT THEIR SUGAR ALLOWANCE FOR THE PRODUCTS ENABLED THE COMPANY TO TAKE ON THE 7-UP FRANCHISE IN THE POST-WAR PERIOD OF RATIONING

the autumn of 1942, the workforce was so shorn that office hours were increased to forty-six a week, and brewery hours to fifty-two a week.

One small item in the Minute Book for 1943 stands out simply because it is so unusual. It was headed "Theft of Beer, T.H.Fraser", and reported that Fraser, one of the draymen, had been found guilty at Acton Police Court of stealing beer from the brewery.

During February 1944 a new danger appeared in the skies: flying bombs. V-1 and V-2 rockets caused random havoc all over London, with the very first V-2 falling in Staveley Road, just round the corner from the brewery. Before the war ended, the brewery itself was hit twice more, with little serious effect. By that time, over seventy Fuller's pubs and off-licences had suffered bomb damage. Despite all this, the company went on making money: the accounts for 1944 show a profit of over £158,000.

The celebrations of VE (Victory in Europe) Day and VJ (Victory in Japan) Day in 1945 gave the brewery a fine opportunity to boost sales yet further. For the former, a special notice was pinned up. It began with a masterly piece of euphemism asking for volunteers: "Owing to the particular position of the Brewing Industry in relation to the public on such an occasion as this, the Directors hope that in order to meet the demands of the situation, a skeleton staff will be willing to work on VE Day and the following day."

So the war was over, and a long period of adjustment and clearing up began. One by one, the serving directors and employees returned from active service to their brewery duties. By 1947, all but seventeen were back in harness. Bomb damaged properties were renovated or rebuilt, though there was little which could be done with the burnt-out Maltings buildings.

The transport department moved tentatively into the age of the internal combustion engine. During 1946 the company bought four new Foden diesel lorries and trailers and a new Bedford lorry. This spelled the

beginning of the end for the ancient steam wagons. No longer could most of the maintenance work be carried out in the blacksmith's shop with hammer and forge. Instead, a more specialized transport garage was set up - though this was very small, and nearly all repairs were done in the open air, regardless of the weather.

By the end of 1948 the "steamers" had gone for good. Bernard Pearce, later to become transport service manager, recalls driving the last of the old wagons to its apparently final resting place in a hedge in Amersham. (After many years, this old faithful was rescued and restored, and can still be seen at rallies in the original Fuller's livery.) Soon afterwards, the Wine and Spirit Department purchased its first lorry. Owing to a shortage of new vehicles, this was an ex-WD truck. "It must have spent some time during the war in the desert," Pearce remembers, "because whenever we had to carry out repairs, we were finding sand!"

This was a time of stagnation. The brewing industry, like everyone else, took a long time to recover from the stresses of wartime, as well as pre-war depression and post-war rationing. Expansion at the Griffin Brewery was slow, and the company had neither the cash nor the inclination for any

bold new enterprises.

The only notable venture of the early 1950s had nothing to do with beer at all. The directors were granted the franchise for manufacturing the American soft drink 7-Up, a process which involved importing a prepared syrup from the USA, processing it and bottling it. At first this was a great success - mostly because of the large numbers of US airmen still serving in or near London. The 7-Up business, run by Gerald Turner

THE TARRING AND FEATHER-ING OF AN APPRENTICE COOPER ON THE COMPLETION OF HIS TRAINING, 1956. THE RITUAL STILL GOES ON IN THE BREWERY TRADE

(R.F.L. Turner's second son), was moved to a new factory on the site of the old maltings. But soon the Americans went home, and a succession of wet summers did nothing for soft drinks sales. Seven-Up, along with its factory, was eventually sold off to a producer of lemonade in 1965.

An altogether happier and more imaginative development took place in 1959, when Fuller, Smith and Turner formed a subsidiary called the Griffin Catering Company. Led by Charles Williams, originally licensee of the Golden Lion at Hillingdon, this ran the brewery's managed houses. The enterprise was expanded still further by Lewis Turner, a future managing director and chairman, who went to the USA to study the way motels were run. His findings were put into practice in the early 1960s, when the Master Robert in Hounslow opened as the first of London's motels. Following Charles Williams' untimely death in 1968, the task of running the catering company was successfully taken over by his son David, now deputy chairman.

This was a straw in the wind. Pubs, and the brewing industry, were beginning to change, and the speed of that change was about to accelerate with bewildering consequences. It was caused by three major elements. One was catering: brewers were realizing that, if the public were going to be enticed into their pubs, they must offer a wider range of food and more attractive surroundings. Fuller's, with its new subsidiary, was well placed to take advantage of the trend. The other two elements were more sinister, however. Giantism was sweeping every corner of British industry, as the big conglomerates swallowed up their smaller rivals. And beer itself seemed to have been transformed. The traditional cask-conditioned product was under massive attack from a brash newcomer - keg beer.

LEWIS JOHN TURNER, FORMER MANAGING DIRECTOR AND CHAIRMAN, NOW PRESIDENT OF FULLER, SMITH AND TURNER

THE MASTER ROBERT HOTEL NEAR HEATHROW WAS FORMERLY LONDON'S FIRST MOTEL (IN 1961). THE ORIGINAL PUB WAS NAMED AFTER THE WINNER OF THE 1924 GRAND NATIONAL. MASTER ROBERT HAD BEEN STABLED NEARBY AT THE PROPERTY OF LYNWOOD PALMER RA, A WELL KNOWN PAINTER OF HORSE SUBJECTS, WHO AGREED TO PAINT A SIGNBOARD DEPICTING THE HORSE ON CONDITION THE PUB WAS NAMED AFTER IT

# Chapter 6

# THE REAL ALE
# TRIUMPH

Cask-conditioned beer is a living thing. Thanks to the traces of live yeast, it continues to develop and change inside the barrel until consumed. This is what makes it interesting. Unfortunately, it can also make it unpredictable and unstable. Cask-, or naturally-conditioned, beer does not generally travel well, and demands a certain skill in storing and handling.

Instability is not something cherished by many manufacturers - especially if a stable alternative is available. In brewing, the only alternative to cask-conditioned beer had always been bottled beer. But in May 1955 a new process was perfected at Flowers' Brewery in Stratford-upon-Avon, producing what was called "bright" or keg beer. It was chemically dead and would last indefinitely, but could be brought to a semblance of life by injecting it with carbon dioxide. Here, surely, was the answer to a brewer's prayer.

Plenty of brewers had been praying hard since the war. Between 1946 and the late 1950s, beer consumption in Britain had dropped from 33 million to 25 million barrels a year. The introduction of death duties had dealt a fatal blow to several family-run firms. Some went bankrupt; others gladly sold out to bigger companies.

The arrival of keg beer did nothing to slow this process. On the contrary, by the early 1960s the new product was making it easier for big companies to succeed: keg beer was easy to transport over long distances, so it could be brewed in larger quantities at fewer sites throughout the country. In 1967, the brewing industry was dominated by just seven giants - Bass, Allied, Whitbread, Watney, Scottish and Newcastle, Courage, and Guinness. They produced nearly three-quarters of all British beer. The rest came from 104 smaller breweries such as Fuller's.

And Fuller's, it seemed, would have to go the way of the rest. Keg was going to take over, and the only way to survive was to embrace it. A tank room for the new "bright" beverage was installed at the Griffin, plus facilities for filtration and flash pasteurization. Hand pumps were removed from the pubs and replaced with an electronic metering system, operated at the press of a button. Besides, the old plant was wearing out. Plans were made to phase out the production of cask-conditioned beer and brew nothing but keg.

But the company's crisis went far deeper than that. Never had it been so near to closing altogether. In November 1968 Lewis Turner, then production director, drew up for the board a discussion document on the future of the brewery. He presented several options. The bleakest of these was to cease brewing entirely and simply operate managed and tenanted houses. The most optimistic option was to build a brand new brewery on the site.

Faced with these stark possibilities, the directors, led by chairman Edward Fuller, were in no hurry to make a decision. Discussions meandered on over the next two years until at last, late in 1970, a compromise was reached: the brewery would be re-equipped on the existing site to increase the production of bottled and bright beers. Next, plans were drawn up, costings made and planning permission sought.

PRESENTATION OF A SILVER SALVER TO EDWARD FULLER BY G F MULLER (CHAIRMAN OF THE TENANTS COMMITTEE) AT THE CLARENDON HOTEL, HAMMERSMITH, 31 OCTOBER 1973. LINED UP ON THE LEFT BEHIND EDWARD FULLER ARE GERALD TURNER (WHO DID SO MUCH TO IMPROVE TENANT RELATIONSHIPS), COL PHILIP STIRLING ELIOT AND LEWIS TURNER. IN THE TOP RIGHT-HAND CORNER ARE: (L TO R) SIR GERARD FULLER, JOHN RUSSELL SMITH, ANTONY ANSELL, ANTHONY FULLER, CHRISTOPHER FULLER AND IAN TURNER. THE SALVER WAS ENGRAVED WITH EVERY TENANT'S NAME

So the months ticked by. But this hesitancy was to prove crucial. While the directors and planners argued and delayed, a consumer revolution was turning the brewing industry on its head. In 1971 the Campaign for Real Ale (CAMRA) was formed, with the aim of showing the big brewers the folly of their ways and ensuring the survival of proper, cask-conditioned beer. To many people's astonishment, the campaign was spectacularly successful. By the end of 1973, there were 30,000 CAMRA members. Sales of "real ale" were soaring, and the products of the smaller, independent breweries had become much treasured and sought after.

ANTONY ANSELL WITH THE REV JOHN YEEND AT THE OPENING OF THE SURVEYOR, WEST MOLESEY, 1974 (NOTE THE KEG BEER DISPENSERS). ANTONY ANSELL HIMSELF WENT INTO THE CHURCH A FEW YEARS LATER

Fuller's took advantage of this shift in public taste, thanks largely to the charm and energy of sales director Antony Ansell (who, with present chairman Anthony Fuller and company secretary Ian Turner, had become a director in 1968). Son of Sir Michael Ansell and Victoria Fuller, he devoted much effort to wooing the campaigners. He listened attentively to their views, and made sure that they were invited to pub openings and other brewery events. As a result, Fuller's became strongly identified with the real ale revolution.

By another lucky coincidence, Fuller's had just introduced a new strong winter brew, ESB, or "Extra Special Bitter", which replaced the extra-dark Old Burton. This struck a resonant chord with beer drinkers. Not only was it one of the strongest regularly brewed draught beers in the country (at 5.5%), it was also one of the tastiest. ESB grew in popularity until it became the Fuller's flagship, and was named CAMRA's Beer of the Year in 1978, 1981 and 1985. (Fuller's London Pride won the accolade in 1979.)

And there was a third stroke of luck. During the late 1950s, the Cromwell Road extension had linked West London with the Great West Road. A major artery, the A4 and (later) the link with the M4, passed right in front of the brewery gates. To countless thousands of motorists, the premises of Fuller, Smith and Turner became a prominent landmark, and the brewery's name one of the most familiar in London. The publicity was worth a thousand advertising campaigns.

By 1974, circumstances had changed dramatically. Sales of bottled and keg beers had slowed considerably, whilst that of draught beer had rocketed. The market for a brewery of Fuller's size

THREE AWARD-WINNING BEERS. FULLER'S HAVE WON THE CAMRA BEER OF THE YEAR AWARD NO LESS THAN FIVE TIMES. THEIR BEERS HAVE BEEN BEST IN CLASS NINE TIMES, WITH ESB VOTED BEST STRONG ALE AN UNPRECEDENTED SEVEN TIMES

and range had been transformed, and the company had to take advantage of this - rapidly. Lewis Turner, the new chairman, realized that greater efficiency was sorely needed in many areas, notably financial matters, which had never been one of Fuller, Smith and Turner's strong points. He brought in a West End auditor called Noel Chambers to overhaul the company's accounting methods. Chambers was an inspired choice. Shrewd, hard-working yet diffident, he eased the erratic cash flow by ensuring that invoices were sent out promptly and regularly, and drew up a new programme of investments and loans.

Sales - and profits - looked rosier by the month. Having taken too long to make their original decision, the directors were now in the happy position of being able to change their minds about the re-development of the plant. Out went the scheme for extending the bright beer production. The space would be used instead for extra storage for draught beer.

The new master plan involved four stages. Phase One, started in 1975, was the most modest, extending the capacity for fermentation, with the installation of eleven conical vessels. This posed a fresh brewing problem. Unlike the old open "squares", which used top-fermenting yeast, they required a yeast which settled on the bottom. After a series of trials, a suitable yeast strain was

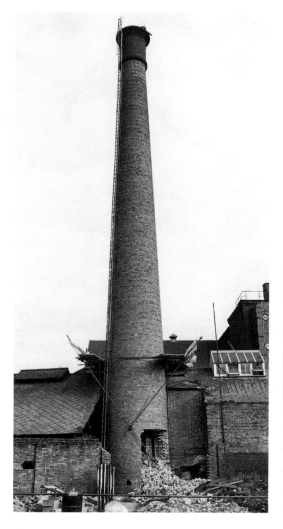

DOWN WITH THE OLD, UP WITH THE NEW. THE BUILDING PROGRAMME WHICH BEGAN IN 1975 TOOK SIX YEARS TO COMPLETE. (*LEFT*) THE OLD BRICK CHIMNEY IS DEMOLISHED. (*RIGHT*) A MATURATION TANK IS SWUNG INTO POSITION OVER THE ROOFTOPS

propagated, enabling brewing to continue with the minimum of disturbance to the original process. A chilling plant and two gas and oil fired boilers were also added, with a new steel chimney replacing the old brick one, which had been a Chiswick landmark for over half a century.

Phase Two was much more ambitious. It required major changes to the brewery site, and thus prolonged attention from the planning authority. Permission was at last granted in July 1978 - almost exactly ten years after Lewis Turner had presented his original document.

So the second stage got under way. By 1980, the new malt storage tower had been completed. Twenty metres high, it was equipped with machinery for handling malt in bulk from lorries, and storing it in four huge silos, each holding 30 tonnes. That April, the new warehouse complex was opened. Covering 4,200 square metres, it was the focus of the new distribution system. Full casks and

kegs were stored here, ready for loading onto the drays, while empty casks were unloaded. The steel floor was covered with thick rubber to soften noise and prevent damage to the casks. The area also housed offices, the cask-washing and racking plant, and a keg-racking plant for the expanding lager market.

A year later the old racking room was converted into a fermentation and tank room. A giant crane swung six conical fermenting vessels high over the rooftops and lowered them into place, where they were soon flanked by twelve maturation vessels.

The new facilities were proudly opened on 28 April 1981. By now, Fuller's had not only a new managing director (Anthony Fuller), but also a financial position of impressive, and growing, strength. Pre-tax profits had climbed above £1 million in 1977 for the first time in the company's history, and sales of draught beer had increased by nearly one third. Profits went on to

DAVID WILLIAMS, DEPUTY CHAIRMAN OF FULLER, SMITH AND TURNER, AND CHAIRMAN OF GRIFFIN INNS LTD (FORMERLY GRIFFIN CATERING)

reach £2 million in 1982, £3 million in 1984 and a staggering £5 million in 1986.

Meanwhile, the next phase of the redevelopment was hurrying ahead, though not without difficulties. The new copperhouse had to be built within very cramped confines, bordered by four existing buildings, one of which was listed. And all the while full production had to carry on around the construction works. New chilled and hot liquor tanks were manoeuvred into place, followed by two wort boiling coppers. These were brought by lorries from Burton-on-Trent (one of which took a wrong turning and wedged its load under a bridge). The copperhouse was officially opened in September 1986 by the local MP, Barney Hayhoe.

The new plant did not just give greater capacity. It also gave Fuller's the ability to brew lager on their premises for the first time. Lager, or rather the British version of it, had made a dramatic rise in popularity throughout the UK in the early 1980s, boosted by aggressive publicity campaigns. For several years the company had bought in Harp lager to sell in its pubs and off-licences. Even with the boom in draught beer, lager had steadily advanced until, by 1986, it accounted for 29 per cent of Fuller's total sales. The time had come for the company to brew its own brand.

FULLER'S REINTRODUCED THIS TRADITIONAL CASK-CONDITIONED MILD ALE IN 1993. HOCK (THE NAME OF THE BEER PREDATES THE GERMAN WINE, SHORT FOR HOCHHEIM, BY SEVERAL CENTURIES) WAS PRODUCED AT CHISWICK IN THE 19TH CENTURY AND BEFORE

A trial lager went on sale in selected pubs during that summer. Enthusiastic noises were made. But what should the new product be called? Inspiration came in rather a bizarre fashion, when a letter arrived asking for sponsorship on behalf of an expedition which was setting out to climb K2, one of the giant mountains of the Himalayas. Sponsorship was given, and Fuller's K2 lager was born. Its launch, however, was clouded by tragedy following the death of two climbers on their way down from the mountain's summit.

Twenty years before, Fuller's had been a struggling local brewery. Now, vast new horizons seemed to be opening up on every side. Bottled ESB Export was being shipped to the United States, where it was sold over a huge area, stretching from Los Angeles and San Francisco to Denver and Houston. When the British Virgin Islands staged a beer festival in 1987, London Pride was the only "real" draught beer available. In July 1990, a deal was signed with the Dutch-based brewers Grolsch, who were eager to import and sell Fuller's beer across the whole of the USA. Round about the same time, Fuller's pubs began stocking Grolsch's draught lager.

THE DISTINCTIVE FACADE OF THE STARGAZEY IN FULHAM ROAD, THE FIRST OF THE ALE & PIE HOUSES - A NEW FULLER'S

CONCEPT WHICH BRINGS TOGETHER TRADITIONAL BEERS AND AUTHENTIC ENGLISH PIES. EACH ALE & PIE HOUSE BEARS THE

NAME OF A TRADITIONAL ENGLISH PIE, IN THIS CASE A CORNISH FISH SPECIALITY

THE INTERIOR OF THE OLD
BANK OF ENGLAND PUB,
OPENED IN AUGUST 1994.
ALONGSIDE THE ROYAL
COURTS OF JUSTICE IN
FLEET STREET, IN WHAT
WAS FORMERLY A BRANCH
OF THE BANK OF ENGLAND,
THIS FULLER'S FLAGSHIP
PUB RETAINS THE
EXTERIOR AND MANY OF
THE INTERIOR FEATURES
OF THE ORIGINAL
BUILDING

Developments at home were even more exhilarating. This was thanks partly, and surprisingly, to the 1989 report on the brewing industry by the Monopolies and Mergers Commission. The Beer Orders which followed the report stated that all breweries with more than two thousand pubs had to sell or free from the tie fifty per cent of the excess over two thousand. It also permitted the tenants of those breweries to buy one cask-conditioned ale from someone other than their own brewery.

The MMC's report and the Beer Orders were bitterly criticized and in many cases damaged trade, with many pubs being forced to close. Yet they brought immense benefit to expanding, medium-sized companies such as Fuller, Smith and Turner. When the big brewers put their excess pubs on the market, Fuller's were on hand to snap up the best of them. In the autumn of 1990, they stunned the brewing world by purchasing no fewer than forty-four outlets from Ind Coope, the pub division of Allied Breweries.

Most of them lay in a swathe extending across Buckinghamshire and Oxfordshire to the edge of the Cotswolds, giving the brewery a well-defined new sphere of influence. Fuller's products would now be directly distributed over a significantly larger area, bordered by the Cotswold Hills, Docklands, Luton and Basingstoke.

The brewery's interests had been growing in another direction all this while. Off-licences had played an increasingly important part in its trade, largely through the inspired efforts of Christopher Fuller (his sure-fire way of expanding the number of outlets was to confront fellow directors with his recommendation for a new site on a Friday afternoon, when they were anxious to get away for the weekend and happy to agree to anything: by the time he retired there were sixty of them), but a growing public taste for wine had produced a demand for something more than the old-fashioned bottle shops.

THE STAR TAVERN, BELGRAVE MEWS WEST. WINNER OF THE
EVENING STANDARD 1992 PUB OF THE YEAR AWARD

FULLER'S QUALITY WINE MERCHANTS AT MAIDENHEAD. THE BRANCH WAS OPENED IN 1973 AND EXPANDED TO DOUBLE ITS
ORIGINAL SIZE IN 1991. THERE ARE NOW MORE THAN 60 FULLER'S WINE SHOPS IN LONDON AND THE HOME COUNTIES

Accordingly, the company off-licences began to be transformed into genuine wine merchants': in some cases, over half the selling space was devoted to wine for the first time. The effect was dramatic. Within a few years, Fuller's shops had become highly respected, not only by customers, but also by wine writers and other members of the trade. In 1992-93, Fuller's were voted "Regional Wine Merchant of the Year" by *Wine Magazine* and the *Sunday Telegraph*. This was the second major award they had won in the space of two years.

The K2 venture came to an end in 1992. There was simply not enough room for storing the lager during its long fermentation and maturation process. Besides which, Fuller's had proved that their real strength lay in brewing traditional English draught ale, something which had earned them an abiding reputation: especially as their products were now widely available as "guests" up and down the land. To replace K2, Carling Black Label was supplied by Bass Brewers; in return, Bass pubs in the South East began stocking London Pride.

The Griffin premises were by now looking less like a building site, as the third stage of the re-building and re-equipping neared its end. The new brewhouse was finally completed in January

ALL IN THE FAMILY: (*L TO R*) IAN TURNER (COMPANY SECRETARY), TIM TURNER, ANTHONY FULLER (CHAIRMAN), MICHAEL

TURNER (MANAGING DIRECTOR), RICHARD FULLER

ANTHONY FULLER, CHAIRMAN OF FULLER, SMITH AND TURNER, IN HIS ROBES AS MASTER OF THE WORSHIPFUL COMPANY OF BREWERS. CHAIRMAN OF THE BREWERS' SOCIETY FOR AN UNPRECEDENTED (IN PEACETIME) THREE YEARS, HE WAS AWARDED THE CBE IN 1990

1993. The old mash tuns, marked as dating from the early nineteenth century, were replaced with new and larger ones, allowing a much-needed increase in capacity. These were installed on the same floor level as the coppers, making it necessary to raise the roof height by four metres. Most of the external walls were clad with reclaimed brick to match the existing buildings.

The story of Fuller, Smith and Turner's first 150 years thus ends on a vibrantly optimistic note, with new plant, new buildings, new outlets and a host of new ideas. It is fitting that this moment has also seen the formation of a new body within the industry, the Independent Family Brewers of Britain. This organization intends to ensure that the needs and opinions of the smaller independent brewers are fairly heard in Westminster and Brussels.

But note the important word in the title: Family. It has been the key to Fuller's survival and success. As Chairman Anthony Fuller says: "Past generations of Fullers, Smiths and Turners created a family firm which thrives today as a progressive and prosperous company, but still with that family image and feeling."

Strong and resolutely independent, with its family traditions intact, Fuller's can look to the future with confidence, led by descendants of the men who founded it long ago.